CLIMBING CROAGH PATRICK

Climbing Croagh Patrick

POEMS BY

Timothy Brownlow

OOLICHAN BOOKS
LANTZVILLE, BRITISH COLUMBIA, CANADA
1998

Canadian Cataloguing in Publication Data

Brownlow, Timothy.
Climbing Croagh Patrick

ISBN 0-88982-172-0
I. Title.
PS8553.R693C64 1998 C811'.54 C98-910935-6
PR9199.3.B72C64 1998

We gratefully acknowledge the support of the Canada Council for the Arts for our publishing program.

Grateful acknowledgement is also made to the BC Ministry of Tourism, Small Business and Culture for their financial support.

We acknowledge the financial support of the Government of Canada through the Book Publishing Industry Development Program for our publishing activities.

Cover image photograph by Timothy Brownlow.

Published by
Oolichan Books
P.O. Box 10, Lantzville
British Columbia, Canada
V0R 2H0

Printed in Canada by
Morriss Printing Company
Victoria, British Columbia

For my wife

Jennifer

"She whispered still that brightness would return"

Acknowledgements

I would like to thank the students in Creative Writing at Malaspina University-College for their invaluable feedback; they helped me find a title and they wrote the blurb for the cover.

Special thanks to my sister, Elizabeth Brownlow Graham, whose tenacious memory and eye for quirky detail, in her oral and written stories, fed my imagination.

Acknowledgements are made to the editors of the following journals and anthologies, in which some of these poems have previously appeared: *The Dublin Magazine, Fleurs du Mal, Hermathena, Icarus, Irish University Review, John Clare Society Newsletter, The Malahat Review, The Oxford Literary Journal, The Penguin Book of Irish Verse, Poems for Clare,* and *Portal.*

"Prelude for Jennifer" was published as a pamphlet in a signed limited edition by Sceptre Press, Northamptonshire.

Contents

All life is exile,

A diaspora of the affections,
A departure of the self from the Self.
They say you can't go home. You carry home

Around with you, you just can't settle in.
What's home anyway? Four opaque walls
Preventing larger views—a mental cage?

Saint Patrick's Day forty years long since. "I
Bind unto myself today" this strength: "God
Bless, my son." My dying father's handshake

Defies the brazen burgeoning of March.
Then I leave up that curving country drive
To lose my father again and again.

Maybe you can go home in gratitude.

The longest road out is the shortest home.

My avocation

Is to celebrate my inheritance.
In Gaelic it is called *dinnseanchas*:
The sacred lore of notable places:

Avoca, The Meeting of the Waters,
Arklow, Tinahely, Aughrim, Carnew:
The crowded signs of boyish cycle trips.

On the Rathdrum road you pass Avondale,
Childhood home of that "sweet blackbird," Parnell.
See the whole country as a palimpsest.

These are the arteries of Narnia,
Paper and pencil my magic wardrobe,
Facts surveyed and contoured into fictions.

Not just in maps do the sweet waters meet.

In winter the milk goes to the cow's horns.

Walking on water

Saint Scóithín passes Barra in his ship:
"How is it you are walking on the sea?"
"It's not sea at all but a flowery field,"

And he picked a purple flower for Barra.
"How is it your ship floats on the field?"
Said Scóithín, whereupon Barra stretched down

Grabbed a salmon and threw it to the saint.
So goes the tenth-century anecdote.
Things haven't changed much: people's agendas

Drive them forward forever cross-purposed.
Or is this about imagination?
You visualise before you see:

Watch those waters blossom, those meadows flow.

Nods are as good as winks to a blind horse.

This is a portrait

Of the artist as developing psyche,
Oaring its miniature submersible
Through the aquarium of tradition,

Testing the limits, exploring the known
To discover the totally unknown:
Knowable without being fully conscious.

This is a handful of word-seed scattered
In half-barrels of rich-soiled potential,
Flowers standing up in their own surprise;

This is a rocket bound for inner space,
Lost microcosms with their Milky Ways,
The apostles carved on one cherry stone.

Take one and let it dissolve in the mind.

Lead your horse to the well; then let him drink.

"My face to the wall,

Playing to empty pockets." Raftery
The wandering bard—celibate and blind—
Rejoices in Mary Hynes's beauty.

Generations later at Ballylee
"I tremble all over thinking of her,"
Whispered an old woman to Yeats. From the roof

Of Thoor Ballylee, the ragged cloudscapes
Of Galway shift their towering cumulus.
From the Martello tower where Joyce once lived

The Baily lighthouse booms and swings its light,
Just as it panned my childhood bedroom wall
Before I learned that words "grow wings or claws"

And build their nests in fortifications.

As the old cock crows, so the young cock learns.

The Saint Anne fugue brings

Memories of Nan, my Irish nanny:
A face like Mother Teresa's, a voice
Indelibly scored for mind-music,

Echoes time-travelling to me like whale-song.
Anne, Nan, Saint Anne, her second name "a rock"
In Gaelic, fortitude her middle name.

How deep the silence with her laughter gone,
Her fiery talk, her whole life a proverb.
Six-sighted when it came to character:

"I'll read him up and down, the amadán,"
And then the verdict, mischievous and sound:
"He's as well up as a car o' monkeys."

Courage like hers makes a clean sweep of life.

An old broom knows the dirty corners best.

A long-lost cousin

Full of anecdotes about family
Turns up one morning. Leaving Dublin docks
The Liverpool steamer passes Howth Head—

"Full of wild garlic." My cousin, homesick
For an Ireland he never really knew,
Sees two tiny figures waving a towel

From the cliff. I peer back forty-five years,
Seeing myself and Nan animated
In a silent movie, grained and jerky.

"Paddy look up be Gaisford's," she would say,
The texture of Ireland packed in a phrase—
Its cliff-echoing birds, its roofless skies—

"It is a hard step for me to leave it."

A friend's eye is the best of all mirrors.

Climbing Croagh Patrick

I pause, in imaginary bare feet,
Swooning, exhausted, taming the monster
Of my inner lusts, my mountainous pride.

Poems are like dragons, the Chinese say,
You rarely see all of them at one glance—
Remember the day driving in Mayo

When I caught a glimpse of Croagh Patrick whole,
Parked the car, adjusted the lens. Too late;
A floating mist obscured the mountain's face.

Always toiling up a steep, shingled slope,
A frail, domesticated Sisyphus,
Practising ways to capture a dragon.

Just look for the flat stones and take your time.

Let not your body encumber your soul.

A fickle creature

Is the Muse. With what arcane contortions
Must the poets court her. Some ritual
Offering seems to be desirable.

Clare jotted thoughts on the crown of his hat,
The scribblings of the yellowhammer's eggs
Perfection he could never emulate.

Wordsworth mumbled along a gravel walk
His massive head groaning with metaphor.
The barks of trees were Hardy's manuscript,

While broken cigarettes lit Yeats's lines.
Milord Byron paced the Newstead cloisters,
A glass of wine each end to keep him sane.

Ploughboy, Laker, architect, mystic, peer.

You don't just plough a field within your mind.

My unborn poems

Crowd mockingly, jabbering about my bed

Or swerve like nimble shoals of tiny fish
Around a small boy's dipping net. Like sand
Trickling out of my tightly clenched fingers

Or raindrops merging on a windowpane.
My words gasp for air but remain deaf-mutes,
Poor damaged foetuses groping the dark,

Legless, armless, double-headed changelings
Daily aborted in the common tide,
Still-born or dragged unwillingly to light.

What a spendthrift life is, scattering seeds,
Prolific wastrel, abundance-maker,
Orchestrator of human pain. There are finer

Fish in the sea than have ever been caught.

"Who will buy poems?"

Complained a seventeenth-century bard
Lamenting his patrons the Fitzgeralds,
And all those who "look up in the sun's eye,"

Giving what the "exultant heart calls good."
First acquire elegance, then the plain style,
Master attention, the key to memory,

The mind empty, "defecated and pure";
Be careful not to swap jade for garbage,
Knowing deep perception is with you,

And deep perception is without you.
"I spare to mention the many kindreds
For whom I might have continued to sing."

Soft words butter no parsnips, but they won't

Harden the heart of the cabbage either.

Lady Gregory

Was told, "Coole is alive with Them, as thick
As grass They are." Sometimes the fairies steal
The butter as it's churning. Here at Coole

The grass is so rich, you could grease your boots,
Grass high and dry from vanishing waters
Honeycombing the underground flowscapes.

The herbs country people say revived Jesus
Also grow here: plantain and dandelions.
Tradition is churning and distilling,

A vat dispensing creamy, fiery sips.
"You must always be drunk," said Baudelaire;
No wonder so many visitors here

Were semantically intoxicated.

There's nothing butter and whiskey won't cure.

"O abbundante

Grazia," cries Dante as Paradise
Unfolds its celestial rose-window,
Rumbles its stage-floor pin-cushioned with stars.

Mankind, this abrasive microcosm,
This billion-times reproduced leaf, can sense
Its partnership with trunk, roots, water, air,

Like a seismograph's needle quivering
As it registers the invisible.
The holy places of the earth vibrate

Our tuning-forks when we are "well-tempered."
"Poetry belongs to those who need it."
I reach my hand to you—"o pioneers"—

Life is a spiral staircase. Hold my hand.

No need to fear the wind with your stooks tied.

Ballykissangel

They call it on a recent BBC show.
My memory mounts a movie dolly
Up the one-street quintessential village.

Swivelling down the drive of Tigroney
The mike crackles with raucous rookeries,
Cacophany of sheep in the distance.

Tea with the Wynne sisters, entrepreneurs
In their eighties; in the hall three silver
Candlesticks await bedtime rituals;

Outside, sheds thatched with outrageous dyes
Shelter crates of local wool for Paris,
Pinks and heathers spirited from the hills.

Scents of gorse and turf. Vale of Avoca,

Every cheek there the colour of foxgloves.

Nineteen fifty-six:

March. We sing my father "across the Bar."
May. Confirmed into the Anglican flock:
I begin my acoustic reformation

Hearing Louis Armstrong's syncopated
Freedom, a tone to shatter glass icons.
Then Aunt Nell's Coolderry—"nook of the oaks."

August. The Edinburgh Festival—
Agincourt in the round with foot-soldiers
Ransacking every corner of language.

December. My mother dispensing gifts,
Our refugee guests inventing a life.
Music, drama, family, growth, and loss.

It takes time to absorb such light and shade.

All in one swig but for the bottle's neck.

"You eat your dinner

And never mind him." My second mother,
Nan, knew that all wisdom was nourishment—
Of the stomach, soul, or head, no matter.

Voices reach me from a childhood kitchen
Recycled by time's seasoned alchemy:
"Good Christ, I'll make him run like a redshank!"

Some insult, actual or imagined,
Had got her goat. Upstairs to "the master":
"Them that's going now's only bits o' ones;

I'll give him boothash." Laughter cures all ill.
So, my father dying all my childhood,
Gossiping with joyful indignation.

What otherworld source did she spring up from?

A wild goose never reared a tame gosling.

In the late 'forties

Just about everything was imported,
Including a hangman. "He's just offa
The boat," cried Nan. As if the Redcoat called

"Walking Gallows" had not done enough work.
The peripheral to-ing and fro-ing
Of dredgers, liners, sailing boats, and tugs

Took on a fearful magic after that.
One night, said Nan, someone stole his kit bag,
Leaving a poor condemned soul in limbo

Until the thief discovered his mistake.
"I thought it was a plumber's bag," he said.
"A quare kind of plumbing he does," mused Nan,

Watching the mailboat pass. "He'll be back soon.

So, here's a double toast to his absence."

"What a fantastic

Yield," exclaimed the visitor at dinner,
My father giving grain by grain the score.
The twenty-acre field had done us proud;

I'd helped plough, harrow, rake and roll it,
The Ferguson tractor my Dinky toy
Painting the green field brown with a slow brush.

Home from school, foot by foot, I'd watched seed leap
Until summer breeze shone shivers down it:
"Orient and immortal wheat." I stood

Dedicating my trials to this sight,
Knowing how hard the earth, how slow the growth,
How few and far between the harvest-homes.

"May my field be munificent as this."

First crack the nuts and then eat the kernel.

One mouth and two ears.

The right ratio. Add two inner ears
For good measure—silent antiphony.
"Whist your spake." You needn't go quite as far

As the monks of Mount Mellory who vow
Perpetual silence. Albert Schweitzer,
Without a keyboard in the jungle, played

Bach through, hitting the middle of the note.
Only in solitary confinement
Can we really hear things in perfect pitch,

Can harness that inner water logic,
Charge that turbine of circular sound waves,
Creating neural electricity.

Negative space. Emptiness speaks volumes.

A silent mouth is very sweet to hear.

Meeting Jacques Prévert

In Paris: he offers me a Gauloise;
We talk: "compositions being performed."
I hand him a battered *Prévert;* he signs;

He spells me Thimotei. Casting a spell
He sketches flowers on the title page,
To keep blooming for me at every turn

Of the leaf: "Sweet present of the present."
He reminds me of Solzhenitsyn's phrase,
"Writers are like a second government."

To Jacques, who looks quite ungovernmental,
After whom most poets are runners-in,
I bow, a poet-haunted constituent,

Letting his words "come to reverberate."

One beetle recognises another.

Three ways of stealing:

Callow poets filch someone else's words,
Clever poets trade bags of ideas,
Good poets break and enter without trace

And what they take is common property.
"Breathing, you invisible poem":
The stealthy rising, falling of slow tides,

Deer tracks imprinted on fresh snow at night,
A watermark lurking beneath the text,
Not invisible, but in-visible.

The more you try to imitate others
The only influence you have is you,
So it makes sense to put it in writing.

"One of a thousand contains all thousand."

Show the calf, not the things that fattened him.

Bicycling in France

I coast down the hill to Ronsard's village;
Dismounting, I saunter into the frame
Of a medieval book of hours:

There is his manor-house, roses and all—
"*Mignonne, allons voir si la rose*"—let's look
Over this wall—what a perfect picture!

A door opens, someone empties a pail;
It's as if one of Vermeer's characters
Put down the letter and said, "Good morning."

Are those oxen clumping down the side-lane?
"Do I wake or sleep?" Which I is this I?
Strange how we're not surprised by perfection;

Perhaps it was indwelling all along.

When God made time he made plenty of it.

Echolocation

Is just one of the tricks that writers use
In triangulating their energies—
Far-asunder barkings from scattered farms.

They explore diverse, ancient parishes,
Townlands, bailiwicks, lost jurisdictions,
Becoming rooted, not parochial.

The mind is a vast echoing-chamber
Of all soundwaves ever reflected there—
How do you fathom those depth-charged waters?

Only by letting the ear take over
Do writers make the visible visible:
They sing the outback into existence.

Delayed acoustics from life's cliff-faces.

Why keep a dog and have to bark yourself?

"Have you ever heard

The one about the Irish lobsters. No?
Well, they're the ones that live in open tanks—
If they try to get out they'll be pulled back."

No wonder we like strangers—a relief
From lace-curtaining each other's actions;
There's always someone who's climbing too high,

Making our puny efforts look absurd.
We develop beady eyes and sharp claws,
Determined that they'll find our own level.

It's the other side of the Celtic soul—
The myth of Finn's gay generosity—
We are indeed generous to a fault.

May God turn the ankles of begrudgers

So that way we'll know them by their limping.

The world inside out

Is what you get when you reverse life's cloth
To explore your own darkest continent—
"Africa and all its prodigies in us."

We expanded first geographically
And seem intent on planet-rape.
Mr. Livingstone, please explore within:

"For I am above Atlas his shoulders."
You'll find mistier waterfalls, jungles
Of multiplying carnage, profusion

Of bird-beasts that would have stumped Linnaeus.
"The only wealth is life." Tailor your needs;
Cull your mental wardrobe of its tatters.

Put on your new coat. Body, mind and soul:

Three folds I have in my seamless garment.

When Saint Columba

Was on the point of death, his big white horse
Approached him, and laid its head in his lap,
Its sad eyes softening mortality.

Iona. Fourteen hundred years ago.
One day a crane sought refuge on the shore
Of that remote island—Saint Columba

Welcomed it, knowing a fellow exile,
And the bird, like the horse, never left him.
The simple life. How hard to emulate:

We who have picked Nature's pockets empty
And switched off the stereophonic stars,
Verbalised the truth that is beyond words.

Be nice to all creatures on your way up;

You'll probably meet them on your way down.

In and out of doors

All one's life. Doors of every colour,
Shape, significance. They make a sound, too.
Always the pantry door of the Old Glebe

Scraped on tiny stones brought in by footsteps;
The door of the coalshed at Ballanagh
Made hollow groans matching darkness within.

Doors literal. Doors figurative. Doors.
Door to the secret garden always locked
However much we leave our longings ajar.

Ceanchor. The flap of the blue kitchen door
Smacks open: Nan, wild-eyed, off the tram—
"Henry's been laid off again on the docks.

Is that justice? Will you answer me that?"

The door to knowledge is questioning.

The magnetic pull

Of joy, of transcending the physical.
"Keep your eye on the ball." Not bad advice.
I yearned to be like great Donald Bradman,

Whose eye was so tuned he played with a stump
Whacking a golf-ball to the boundary;
Four inches of willow and a big ball

After that was like playing telescope.
"Such, such were the joys"—the parabola
Of that rapidly deflected spinner

Seeking its destiny in my open palm,
My privileged hand instinctively prompt.
"What we play is life": *Homo ludens*

Knowing God between his shoulder blades,

The Holy Ghost keeping an eye on him.

"Where did you get her?

She's as good a laugh as Jimmy O'Dea."
Laughter. Another thing gone out of style,
As irrelevant, let's say, as the Thais

Floating little candle-boats out to sea
Freighted with their guilts, worries, and nightmares.
A local lad had roughed up my brother;

Nan stomps up to the club house, indignant:
"Are you Liam O'Connell?" "I am, so."
"Take that, you bandbeggar." She sweeps her hand.

"I gave him a clather; he's fallin' yet.
Six months elapsed. You wouldn't credit it
But Liam tells me he's gettin' married

And there'd be no show without yours truly."

Let your anger go with the setting sun.

I open the shed:

A frightened bird ricochets to freedom.
Another day, I rescue a handful
Of throbbing life—a snow-grounded starling.

Releasing them, we deconstruct our pride.
"Don't they make their nests very nice and snug,
And they never get instruction from God,"

Said Oisín in his tryst with Saint Patrick.
My mother told me that during the prayers
At my father's deathbed, the canary

Kept to distract my father from his pain
Revised the words with soul-piercing descant,
Music meeting Word wingtip to wingtip.

"There is not one note too many in it."

The song of the high, ever-living birds.

"I am not only

[Poetic] in myself but also cause
Of [poetry] in others." Falstaff's wit
Feeds off itself, giving others ballast.

So Clare trespasses universal pastures,
Stands a scarecrow in imprisoned fields,
Sprouting extra eyes like an old potato;

While biddable poems flock to his hand,
Patient Saint Francis pours redemption
Of rural brotherhood and sisterhood.

Once misspelled "The Northamptonshire pheasant,"
He hides in the ditches for fear of guns,
Wings exploding into song-freighted air.

The patron saint of modern poetry.

An often-used pitcher breaks in the end.

We leave the Welsh coast:

"There's Wicklow Head"; my hungry eye swivels
The panorama, unscrolling my past:
"There's the Big Sugarloaf, and the Little,

Lugnaquillia, Vallombrosa, Lambay,
Howth, Katigollaher, Poulaphuca,
The Hell Fire Club, the Castletown folly."

What goes around, comes around. No matter
From how far, the spirit comes home to roost;
Those balsa planes with paraffin engines

We launched into hope always circled back;
The model yacht scudding out in rough sea
Tacked home. We take off over fields light-rinsed.

Roll up that scroll. "Until we meet again,

May God keep you in the palm of His hand."

What is writer's block?

Refrigeration, stasis, still water.
It can last twenty minutes or ten years;
The more one forces it, the more it sticks,

The more you blow the sparks in that black grate
The more you look like those pot-cheeked cherubs
At the corners of old maps. Coleridge

Took opium for fear of it, Wordsworth
Perambulated every mountain path
To keep his head above it. Marcel Proust

Celebrates those *intermittances du coeur*
Whereby emotions are time-capsuled
To release their buried secrets years on.

Lift your head from the block—"relish versing"—

The deep peace of the flowing air to you.

In the Vatican

They jealously guarded a manuscript—
The only one—Allegri's *Miserere*—
A sound only fit for angels and monks,

Locked and padlocked behind musical bars,
Those timeless pauses evaporating
Upwards, not to be grounded in the mind;

Until one day in Rome the floating notes
Found a rest in the capacious inner
Ear of a young visitor's attention.

When he got home, Mozart coaxed those song-birds
Down from their giddy perches, uncaged them
And released them into the common air.

Unlock your mental Vatican to write

The good, the merciful, the singing word.

The silver restored

To its rightful owner, Nan leaves the court:
"You've been a marvellous witness." "Indeed,
I did your work," she quips to the Garda.

She had given chase in a white squad car
That morning, catching the tinkers off guard—
"Don't make a fashion of that, me buckos."

Later, on a visit to Jervis Street
Hospital, she sees one of the tinkers:
"Jesus, Mary, and Joseph, they'll murder

Me now." So she burns the purple outfit
She was wearing as she played detective.
Policing her beat around Sutton Cross,

Nan restored silver to these leaden times.

Better to be quarrelling than lonesome.

Anna Livia

Plurabelle: Joyce's dear, dirty Liffey;
Yeats's Garavogue, foaming through the weir
At Sligo, peat-tinctured water like stout.

Rivers of Ireland, meander through me,
Recollect my scattered pebbles, polish
With your gravitational momentum

Those multiple-hued, submerged glimmerers.
From what hidden mountain springs do you come,
Taming your timeless gurgling energies

On the frozen plains of my upsilted veins?
There is no tributary lost. Avon
Mór and Avon Beag, Avoca, Dargle,

Blackwater, Nore—"O, could I flow like thee!"

Frost, ice, and snow are nothing but water.

Thirty-two counties

In geography, if not in history.
"We haven't joined the world yet. We are still
In the embryo," says a Dublin man.

"Enchanting"; "as narrow as a pig's back."
Take your pick. Ireland can be both at once,
And so you don't really have to decide.

Better to sit in what MacLiammóir
Called "pan-faced reverie" over the pint,
Join Kavanagh's "standing army" of bards,

Always just about to flourish the pen.
"Much better to remain outside the world;
As if they haven't made a balls of it!"

Flann O'Brien, where are you when we need you?

Here's to the light heart and the heavy hand.

The Irish triads

Celebrated the mystic rule of three,
Three-pronged forks composting cultural soil.
Saint Patrick surely had the common touch

Showing a shamrock for the Trinity,
Explaining Three in One and One in Three.
Silently playing trio sonatas,

My hands pursue two distinct registers
My feet fast-pedalling me down to earth.
Even music cannot be pure. Human

Destiny is a tripartite puzzle
From darkness through darkness into darkness.
"The ould triangle goes jingle-jangle,"

While on an abandoned hill stand three trees.

We forgive greatness when it's safely dead.

Talking to a friend

Who breeds Irish Draught horses: "I give them
Instructions at night so they sleep on it;
Somehow next day they know what you have said."

At the Irish National Stud, horses
Sleep standing under skylights, absorbing
The slow configurations of starlight,

Constellations of thoroughbred promise.
State-of-the-art vitamins are just part
Of a quick-witted, sure-footed stardom.

It's hard enough to tell the sheep from goats
These days—you're not meant to be judgmental.
Sheep are good but passive, goats mischievous:

"Not one without damage or roguery."

A goat's beard is not a fine stallion's tail.

What is poetry?

Housman didn't dare shave thinking of it,
Dickinson felt like it was eternal
Cold or the top of your head coming off.

It's what gets lost in translation, the *crème*
De la crème, primal, unreasonable;
Like freedom, in constant need of defence.

Impossible to define. Without it
All definitions would lose precision,
All dictionaries not worth swallowing.

Emanating a kind of chlorophyll
Keeping tolerable the air we breathe.
Each poet magnifies the sacred grove:

Listen to the voice of those wind-swept woods.

The trees remain, the planters disappear.

"Imagination

Dead. Imagine." Language must have roots,
Branch out in all directions to blossom,
Exfoliate in joyous energy.

Words are like money, they earn interest,
They have a purchase on reality.
They are also quicksands of inflation

Wrapping up experience in slickness.
"Money, Thou art a powerful master."
Hard not to become obsolete these days

When words go out of fashion like old shirts,
And no-one wants to see the Emperor.
Facile words herd up in cliques like people,

Driving the black sheep of meaning away.

Scabby sheep like to have scabby comrades.

Nothing like a thump

On the head to restore one's natural voice.
The story goes that Donald Trump's mother
Was mugged and started talking gibberish.

Things were going rather badly for her
Until someone noticed she was speaking
Gaelic, restored to her traumatically.

Quite a metaphor for modern culture,
Where to talk in one's native dialect
Is to be taken for an imbecile.

Old languages are like old instruments,
As Stradivari knew when he made
Violins that seem to remember sound,

Articulating hidden vibrations.

Old and seasoned pipes give the sweetest smoke.

Returning from France

A quarter of a century ago.
Good Friday in Notre Dame de Paris:
"Seigneur, Tu sais tout, Tu sais que je T'aime."

Glimmer and soar. Canterbury next day.
Easter Sunday in Westminster Abbey—
The only place left that has a corner

For poets—a community of dust.
Who says there is no modern pilgrimage?
When one loves "as an emerald is green,"

No act of attention is lost. Poets
Heal the ancient rift between word and Word
By seeing everything unfragmented.

Three shrines; two religions; one investment.

What good's an umbrella with leaking shoes?

There are no short cuts

To quality. Might as well ask Chardin
How he works quotidian miracles
Or how skies with weightless lovers struck Chagall.

Try this on for humility: Mozart
Wrote six hundred works in as many months—
Not much time for dreaming when every breath

Converts the mundane air into marvels.
Johann Sebastian, synthesizer,
Whose notes make perfect circles in the sand,

Who voices the abyss, soul-acrobat
Who blends, unlocks minor and major keys
Of mortal, terrestrial, fallen things,

Bridging our frayed hand-me-down silences.

If you lie down with dogs, you'll rise with fleas.

Christmas '89

Half a million Irish people come home
To where the trees are always whispering
Of a life in themselves and yet beyond.

Nan, her hip broken, is "giving out"—"Good
Turkey? It's as hard as the hobs o' hell."
I visit the bar where she had standing

Orders—"Here's herself"—a Paddy and Red
Was slid down the counter like a Western.
The barman shakes my hand again, again:

"So Nan is gone, Nan is gone, Nan is gone.
When you were born, a light lit up her heart;
She always waited for you to come home."

At her bedside, I watch life's mysteries

Lighting the light—putting out the light.

Delivering mail

With Leo McGlew, the lanky postman,
I got to know the Baily inch by inch,
Gorse clicking in the heat, long flights of steps,

My unconscious sandals growing wings.
Drumleck, The Needles, Edros; Roxboro
Where they blew a whistle to summon staff.

Our route was a thread through a human maze;
Why did I neglect to pocket that spool
To lead me back from many rocky paths

Back to the fug of the tiny office
Where the postmistress had all the gossip
Gleaned from listening to every phone-call?

"Commire till I tell you, d'you know who's dead?"

The fox found himself the best messenger.

"Will get you nowhere

Fast, that poetry lark." Hard to refute.
It will not save your money or your soul;
Dictators and bureaucrats don't like it,

So why do you keep committing it?
Habit, stubbornness—a longing to still
The perpetual transience of things

In the developing fluid of words.
Watch those negative images emerge
And float triumphantly in metaphor.

Pace Sigmund Freud, art is not disease;
It is a slow, patient recovery
Of all that entropy can dissipate.

Long live syntactical convalescence!

All patients are doctors after their cure.

"My curves are not mad"

Said Matisse, his loaded brush hovering,
Tracing ghostly paradigms of a face,
Air-conditioned before they touched canvas.

In wheel-chaired age, he had his work cut out
Juggling space between work and laziness.
Our modern culture is disembodied,

As if our heads, our hands, our hearts, our feet
Inhabited different compartments;
It's time we took up connectedness.

But Matisse gets under the skin of time,
Observing things as if he was not there—
A face, a chair, a fruit, the Vence Chapel—

Reinventing the nature of nature.

He who would be chief, let him be a bridge.

There are no answers

Only the right questions. You might as well
Wheel out smoke in a net-and-wire barrow
As get a grasp of truth, reality.

Look. When masts enter a new element
They snake, wobble in liquid abandon,
Figments of their own imaginations.

When we live at the centre of our light,
Pale moons reflections of that greater blaze,
We help its journey across the heavens,

Our hard, glassy egos refrangible.
And you, river, how does it feel to touch
Our frail amplifiers with your music?

This is the promised land, we are on time.

Chase Nature off and she returns, running.

Imagine virtue

As its own content. To do a thing well
Is to hit an invisible bull's-eye,
To mindmap an elusive horizon.

Vertiginous prayers of Skellig Michael
For God and for the birds. Anonymous
Sculptors high on the roof of Notre Dame

Skylighted by celestial birdsong,
Not caring if their work was ever seen,
Escaping the erosion of millions

Of hungry eyes—the Mona Lisa's look
Of do-not-touch-me wariness, of a face
Eyeballed so often that it disappears.

"Excess is the absence of energy."

It is for her own good that the cat purrs.

Bike against the fence,

I held the small box-camera steady
As the lumbering DC-3's groaned in.
In those days, even high technology

Had a human face. The pilot waved down.
I'd cycled there from Howth, many thousands
Of miles notched up on the odometer.

Remember the thrill of hitting forty
On the speedometer; the landing planes
Were not that much faster then. The Howth tram

With its Cyclops eye—fifteen miles per hour—
You had to duck the branches as they veered
Towards the open caged-in seats on top.

Slow-motion shots from Bray to Ireland's Eye.

Slip into Heaven while the Old Boy nods.

Beatrix Potter's

Tale of Peter Rabbit was once described
As the "quintessential English novel."
I agree. Such Lilliputian shrinkage!

Imitations are always popping up—
Plot, character, syntax, rhythm, menace,
Alliteration, humour, direct speech,

Parody, onomatopoeia, style—
Are just a few virtues that get lost.
"Nature's chief masterpiece is writing well."

Measure twice, cut once; weigh each word on scales,
"Aim for the bull's-eye but don't get stuck there."
With such paradigms, such microcosms,

Why invent new models of yesterday?

Forsake not old friends for passing fancies.

For the Book of Kells

One hundred and forty calves were killed. Called
"Chief treasure of the western world," pages
Of vellum still show hair side or flesh side.

Up the creaking oak stairs of Trinity
Long Room, a tourist to my past, I stare,
Intuiting four gospels from one page:

The man, the lion, the calf; the eagle
Who stares at the sun without being dazzled.
Two little men contest the letter "N,"

Pulling beards in divided loyalties.
"Mine heritage is like a speckled bird."
From Pangur Bán, the scholar-poet's cat,

Learn how to hunt words without eating them.

Scholar's ink lasts longer than martyr's blood.

Twiddling the loose knobs

Of my ancient radio, suddenly
Clarity speaks out, besieged on all sides
By babble, crackle, sad static voices.

Hunger for audible calibrations!
So many things conspire to interfere,
Making the normal channel so much noise.

Space is not the only absence, but time.
There must be a place where past voices go,
Or is my set too crude to pick them up?

Stay tuned. Your past is coming on the air.
"This is your life," it says. Do not switch off.
Dim your mental egocentricities:

Firelight won't let you read, but it is warm;

Besides, you won't see the dust on the floor.

Vasari tells us

That when Donatello made a statue
He pleaded before it, "Speak, damn you, speak,"
That Raphael painted Pope Julius

So lookalike that everyone trembled,
That Brunelleschi rigged giddy canteens
High on his Dome to keep the builders fresh,

That this excitement "in the very air
Of Italy" was spiritual plankton
Purging people's minds of former grossness.

As whales feed, canvas breathes, stone utters,
Sow your words, poet, for posterity,
To connect past with radiant present.

Slice into hidden furrows of knowledge,

The frame of your plough a handful of pens.

"Only in Ireland"

As the fella says. The token Catholic
On the staff of an Anglican college:
"And where did you spend your holidays, Lodge?"

"I went to Lourdes, ma'am," his eyes lighting up.
"Oh, did you see the Australians batting?"
I often replay that moment at Lords:

Denis Compton sweeps—"Ashes for England!"
Just opposite that tawdry cinema
Stood a monument to the Ninety-Eight.

They left a different kind of ashes here;
Not much time for cucumber sandwiches
At the clash of irreconcilables.

Framed cricketers in immaculate whites.

Her own chicks appear white to the raven.

John Synge on Aran

Didn't have the brogue: "a shoe on the tongue."
His Gaelic was slow but impeccable,
It was his heavy boots that let him down

As he watched bare-footed children clamber
The rocky promontories with their toes,
Their hard-soled insteps nonchalant as birds.

Gaelic fell with soft imprints around him,
Its timeless intonations never shod
With the leathery numbness of logic.

You can't unlearn your inheritance,
Best to preserve what innocence you can.
He takes his last, hammers, pulls, and fashions

Rhythms to fit the most intrepid foot.

Buckles are great additions to old shoes.

Ave atque Vale,

Dear presence, dear absence, dear guardian
Of my rhapsodies, stitching me together;
One more resurrection, and then adieu.

Let's go back fifty years: forty-seven,
When music went round on seventy-eights,
And the craze was dances from the Twenties.

My sister had set the scene: long hallway,
Wind-up gramophone, slanting evening sun;
She was vainly trying to learn the Charleston

When round the corner you flung yourself,
Showing a parable with your timing—
Now a slow-motion playback forever.

"The roars of her; we were crippled laughing."

If you can't laugh at yourself, get a mirror.

Poets and grownups

Was how Cocteau divided us all up.
The more "grown-up" I get, I see he's right.
Some people grow grey hairs in their cradle,

Some others are like "refugees from time,"
They keep doors open, windows wide, turrets
Of hope surveying eternal landscapes.

So build poets, unlicensed architects,
Stanza by stanza creating mansions
Cellar to attic in blueprinted air,

Not one brick fired in an expected kiln,
Firm foundations releasing "window songs."
Thus may I make my house of poetry;

Maybe one day I will inhabit it.

It is no use boiling your cabbage twice.

Disappearing things:

Frisky deer blending into undergrowth,
Ants into woodwork, fleas into cat's fur,
Last year's leaves into grass, grass into soil,

Light into twilight, raindrops into water,
Violas into strings, cream into milk,
Money, happiness, most relationships,

Wind into stillness, thoughts to memories,
Salt into soup, butter into pancakes,
Promises into air, waves into sea,

The helicopter seeds of sycamores,
Shooting stars, my mother's head thrown backwards
In never-again ecstatic laughter.

Count humdrum blessings. A trout on the plate

Is better than a salmon in the sea.

Let's make a collage:

Come in, we're open; no bicycles please;
United colours of; pure honey;
Members and guests only; passenger zone;

Welcome to Julia's place; Sweet'n low;
These premises are leased by; Killer Loop;
Erected 1903; 3 minute max;

Advanced night repair; pleasures for men; stop;
How was our service today?; ezebrew;
Do not block driveway; we've got you covered;

Free map; the new American fragrance;
Limited vision; sale; thanks for the brake;
Attitude is a five-letter word: Irish;

Control the destiny of your skin;

Walk softly on the earth; we'll match the price.

This is a letter,

Mater dulcissima, to you. I know
You are beyond the reach of Mercury,
Where words no longer carry their own weight,

Where you "Fear no more the heat o' the sun":
Your favourite Shakespeare. My favourite
"Calls back the lovely April of [your] prime."

My love is ancient, a rough-hewn passage
Tomb which waits millennia to be lit
By dawning light at the winter solstice.

Much as I miss your enchanted letters,
Your voice "in the temple of my hearing"
Is a kitchen clock unaware of time.

You know how to turn gravity to grace.

Adieu, addio, *dulcissima mater*.

In County Wicklow

Now, farmers are taking out their harrows,
Hot stallions are covering their mares,
While the "coloured counties" change their colours.

Think of Itchiku Kubota who makes
A sequential landscape with kimonos—
You hang it up like a magic clothes-line:

Freshly laundered vestments of memory,
Flapping, swaying, billowing into sails,
Tangy to the nostrils like new-baked bread.

Thus may my garments congregate the line,
Relaxed but not slack, taut but not rigid,
Each one re-membering my former self.

One day I'll even throw away the pegs.

Here's to a wet night and a dry morning.

"The Long Memory"

Was the title of the movie that night;
As we entered the drive of Ballanagh
We had a row about the gate, who was

To shut it. They say that the mind edits
As it goes, unconsciously proofreading
The painful scribbles of experience—

Geniuses as we dream, if nowhere else.
Forty years later, I stand at that spot—
A speaking ghost in a Hardy poem.

The old Irish country gate still stands there,
The squeal of its rusty white hinge swirls me
Into a sudden "land of lost content."

Now I say, "Father, the gate is open."

The deep peace of the quiet earth to you.

II

Les Coquelicots

This picture of all others rules my days,
Claude Monet's painted poppy-littered field,
   That changeless summer day
Which never was. The restless light displays
Four figures on the bank, the meadow grasses
   Whitened by the breeze,
While in one corner, by a clump of trees
A sudden cloud has drowned the field in shade
But sets the pink tiles of the house ablaze.

A young girl with a parasol is seen
At first, and near her stands a dreaming child.
   A reckless splash of blue
Reflects the sky. The painter's eye can scheme
And regulate his patterns; though the air,
   Already turning cold,
Will drive him home, his memory will hold
Impressions of a thousand other days
To recreate this evanescent scene.

So art transforms with such a fragile power
Accumulated sorrow and lost joy,
   And finds the hidden centre
Where Eastern scriptures say the lotus flower
Blooms amid a landscape where no time
   Can break its slender stalk.
Imagined and unreal, these figures walk
Through summer days we all have known, giving
Darkness its true light, and sunlight its brief hour.

Ars Poetica

Lady Jane Grey, Foxe reports, when denied pen and ink in the Tower, managed to scratch out a poem with a pin.

J. W. Saunders: *The Profession of English Letters*

Like the clusters of angels on the head of this pin
My head must keep its equilibrium
Though far from angelic

This is economy, distillation
They may not find it for a hundred years
The usual time lag

The last rays glide over my manuscript
Illuminating this curriculum mortis
My dark chamber

The wall is stained like Leonardo's
Would it were glass so that it might transmit
Not just absorb

I am writing for all I am worth
With this pin I prick their consciences
Don't lose your head

Craftsmanship

(Saturday 27th March 1802: At Breakfast Wm. wrote part of an ode. Mr. Olliff sent the dung and Wm. went to work in the garden.)

Journals of Dorothy Wordsworth

A good day for William; the ode
Has begun to sprout, and now
He lays aside his pen for spade,

And feeds the all-absorbing ground
As carefully as he imbibes
The sustenance of sight and sound.

The gardener knows just how much oil
The hidden wicks will need before
They are rekindled in the soil.

Much dung, few roses, every age.
He goes indoors to find his poem
In full flower on the page.

St. Columba and the Bards

Back from Iona, bare of trees and birds,
He now tramps wider pastures strewn with herds,
Their lowing tells him that he is at home:
Hills silhouetted on the sky as some
Demented artistry steeps all afresh
Each hour in changing tones, sets them awash
In liquid outline, fades them into haze,
And swells the hidden wood dove's throat with praise.
Each hedgerow after rain seems filled with song,
Each bush a diadem of light. "We wrong
The poets if we wrench away this joy
Of pagan fellowship. We can destroy
With careful breath or careless hand the bond
Built up between each creature and the land.
Make the outer inner, and the inner
Outer, so all in Christ's clear eye, sinner,
Poet, priest, prince and child regain their sight."
A blackbird called, he stood transfixed by light.

Portrait

She paces mindlessly her shuttered room,
An old rook straying among winter trees,
Whose blatant intricacies of dead bloom
Recall her careless eye from fantasies.

A dead child's faded clothes and shoes confess
What might have been, are objects which decline
Through every syllable of loneliness,
Her soul, caged by capricious nets of time.

When light enters, as her nonchalant hand
Allows it, with flick of withered curtain,
Tinges with habitual love each strand
Of hair, its gaze reveals her furtive den.

Startled eyes, like a stoat pinned on a stake,
Wedged in her skull, where God's candles confer
No sacrament, tell of her plight. Pray, break
Bread for her darkness, which no love can stir.

Father and Son

A new element now entered into my life, a fresh rival arose to compete for me with my Father's dogmatic theology. This rival was the Sea.

Edmund Gosse

The rock pools tinkled
As my Father's hammer
Clacked the virgin acres
Of that amphibious world
Sea pinks budged
Anemones sighed

I remember one pool
Which will forever hold us
Reflected in negative
(Clouds drifted in reverse)
My Father's image
And my childish moon
Catching his light at one remove

The rising tide
Would one day pour into that pool
My lunar transformations
O harsh eclipse
O treacherous iconoclastic Sea

Hedge School

It seems as if all nature is on strike,
The land stripped bare of trees. The priest well knows
The likes of him can dangle on a pike.

He teaches here, his instinct on its toes
Like any fox, without more shelter than
The fields where silent badgers search out sloes,

And stoats and weasels squabble like old men.
The scarecrow flock repeat with reverence
His words "Through Jesus Christ Our Lord, Amen,"

Or parrot after him pounds, shillings, pence,
Or last week's Latin or a Gaelic rhyme,
And hold for twenty minutes hunger in suspense,

Until the stormy clouds proclaim it's time
And rats take over the deserted scene.
Redcoats permeate the landscape, and climb

On every wall and ruin to scour it clean.
The tallest of them, "Walking Gallows," jerked
A dozen priests out of their Papist dream

Last week, and does not look too overworked.
Nearby, in murky light, the priest says Mass
And blackened lips respond; no care is shirked

In this wide parish, souls without compass,
Proud hearts rudderless, minds bereft of sail,
(They crouch like animals as soldiers pass),

All happiness evicted without bail,
Their prayers addressed to Cross, crown, scourge, and nail,
Whose Rebel dies, like them, beyond the Pale.

Mindscapes

I stand before my pupils
And recite by heart.

Letters drift from punctual moorings,
Fluttering, rising
Off the page, sudden birds
Swerving and regrouping
In windswept knots,
Melting traceries,
Filling the surprised sky
With dissolving syllables.

You've heard of icebreakers—
Even the laggards at the back
Lift their heads and stare.

Drifting flocks of words
Alight on the breathless surface,
The nonchalant imprints
Of relaxing ripples
Are briefly refracted
In sixty pairs of dilated pupils
Focusing inwards.

Learning by heart.

Prelude for Jennifer

Rain falls on fallen foliage of my mind
As on the trees. The stricken roots grope down
Exploring clay and moving stones to find

Renewal. Gestures, smiles, unspoken words
Are littered leaves, the mind made sharp by loss,
As this stark tree remembers leaves and birds.

I dedicate these words to you, my dearest,
Not out of any misplaced sense of pride
Or affectation, for trees are nearest

Symbols of the way my poems grow.
You are my sun and rain. You make my sap
Defy the laws of gravity. I know

At times an oaken strength, at times the beech
Is emblem of my scattered twigs, or ash
My trembling limbs, or yew my lack of speech.

Now is the solstice of my winter mood
And I have bared myself to take the light.
Hail, rain or snow, replenish me for good.

Seagulls

Seeing seagulls stroll about the sky
In nonchalant gyrations
The old man stoops, halts by
Hedge and railing, and shuns
The thought sketched out
For him against the clouds.
He must, however, scout
This once, the memory which shrouds
Irrelevancies and some truth.
Of such is his experience,
That he, once a stubborn youth
Grown poetic in a sense,
Feeling such delirium
Of new-found energy
As must, under this same sun,
Have stirred complexity
In the simple heart
Of Icarus, dropped unheard
From cloud to wave, his art
And dream the image of a bird.
His fate, perhaps, is worse

To know that these ironic birds
Have power to mock his cause
With brainless, soaring words.
Bright-eyed Icarus never saw
This curse, his tragic body
Slipping silent down the raw
Ocean. He had no time to study
How, before the surface smoothed
Where, falling, he surprised it,
The gulls had shrieked, soothed
In vengeance, the turmoil of their hate.

Thomas Bewick: Woodcutter
(1752-1828)

You bow and scrape
Superfluous wood
It's sometimes hard to see the trees

Long weeks of labour
To liberate the block
A life's work against the grain

Twig by twig
The filigree emerges
Through the wrong end of a telescope

Your gaze bifocal
Your perspectives true
Spontaneity the twin of patience

Papageno
Your birds are caged in wood
Set them free in relief

The fowler's gun
A bird's-eye view
An infinite wariness is desired

Such moving stillness
If we come too close
Your birds will all fly away

John Clare and Picturesque Landscape

PARADISE PLACE. Spring guns and steel traps are set here.
Cobbett, *Rural Rides.*

You are sometimes seen on your hands and knees,
Or sleeping out, where high flocks of geese

Are initialled on your mind's window ledge.
You forage the grasses, probe every hedge,

Overtures to Love lovingly rehearsed,
A "shy come nightingale," "so rudely forc'd."

Snipe are your emblems of joy, Paradise
Bumbarrels peppering the windy skies.

Then you are visited, a tourist's delight,
You mutter greetings, and hide from their sight.

Strangled moles, steel traps, and that rifled nest
Convince Arcadia is sham at best.

Your friends are hunted, but they have no tongue.
Peasants, like pictures, can be framed and hung.

James Clarence Mangan in Trinity College Library

His weary eyes watch lanterns in the square
Squeak in wind, papers blown about the air,

Great trees dishevelled by the sudden squall,
Which woke him from his dream behind the wall

Of books, bound books that he knows little of
Except the few which fire his frenzied love

And keep him from his cataloguer's task,
(And like the busts, his face a pallid mask.)

The snug alcove where he preferred to work
Was near the sightless gaze of Swift and Burke,

But his rage was of other kind than theirs.
Stiffened with alcohol, he sought the stairs

And stumbled out of eighteenth-century grace,
Across the cobbles, dreaming of a race

As yet unborn, or dead so long he saw
The merest ghosts emerge from history's maw,

And racked by drugs and dreams, like Baudelaire,
He walked the city of his heart's despair,

Across the river, up to his dark den,
And lit his candle, coughed, took up his pen

And wrote some verse that morning would not spare
(The pale sky showed the dawn already there)

Until, defeated, he snuffed out the flame
And with it seemed to blow away his fame.

Tomorrow, Berkeley, Swift, glue, ink and dust,
And madness winking at him from a bust.

In Memoriam W.H. Auden

Christ Church Cathedral, Oxford, 27th October, 1973

The force of gravity has got you down
At last; simple now your eroded frown

Of a face, your radar eyes no longer
On the watch for every sort of danger.

You kept our cities clean, our suburbs free
From cant and lies (metaphorically),

As every poet, had a nose for words,
Loved hanging round them, fed them crumbs like birds

To breed sweeter songs. Poetry is faith,
Not as the text books say, but kin to death,

Which is what Christ, as you acknowledged, said.
And that is why we're here. You are not dead,

But live in a perspective without weight,
Annihilating flesh, time, words and hate.

You gain the stillness of the moving notes
Which music draws from all-too-human throats.

If ever dove descended, it is here,
(Or harmony was cajoled from its sphere,

If ever Orpheus made lovers weep
Or stones obeyed Amphion's lyre to leap

Into their place), it is among us now.
And St. Cecilia's Hymn reminds us how

Mozart fainted when he first heard the horn;
Though far from fainting now, our minds feel shorn

Of all pretence, our egos beaten flat.
(What modern artist has done more than that?)

"No man is an island"; single ice floes
Mingle, fuse into archipelagos

Of human patterns. We could do much worse,
You say, than learn how strength can conquer force.